PLANTED TREE

Creating His PATH To Freedom

www.LivingByPreceptsMinistries.org

livingbyprecepts00@sbcglobal.net

ISBN 978-0-9790926-4-0 *paperback* 978-0-9790926-4-7 *epub*

DEDICATION

When I started this project almost eleven months ago, an incredibly wise mentor said, "Ma, write your heart-story. I promise that I will buy the first copy of your book."

Although my mentor has since moved to her heavenly home, I can still clearly hear her clarion mandate. "Ma, write your heart-story." So, I dedicate this book in honor of my dear daughter and thank her for pushing and stretching me to finish this book. She realized that by penning and sharing my story, my broken heart would heal and beat again.

To our late daughter, Amoyiah, or as we called her, The Doctor. She always seemed to know how to encourage my heart at exactly the time I needed it most. She always thought she had the answer to every situation. She knew what was best for me and everyone else. She just knew I should pick up the phone by the second ring when she called, and she insisted on sending me gifts, or as she liked to call them, "gifticees." She never needed a reason or a special occasion and she always said, "Just because." I am so honored to dedicate my story to her.

She called me early in the morning on the day of her home-going to see the King. The call went something like this: "Ma, what you doing?"

I rubbed my eyes and replied, "Amoyiah, it is 3:23 a.m. and you ask me what I'm doing?"

I was busy hosting a Christian women's conference that weekend, so I was not even at home in my own bed. If I had known this would be the last time I would hear her voice on this side of heaven, I would have allowed her to ask all the same questions over and over again.

For all you mothers who have lost a child and have walked this same painful journey, I pray my story will encourage you to love unconditionally and to always take the time to pray for, honor, respect, bless, love, listen to, discipline, and cherish your children. I pray that you will count every moment as precious.

Amoyiah, you were our one-of-a-kind daughter and forever your daddy's little girl. Our daughter, take your rest. We long for the day when we can hold you in our arms and see you again face to face. We love you, Punkin'! We thank our heavenly Father for the honor of being your parents. You will always be forever in our hearts, and I dedicate this book to your memory.

TABLE OF CONTENTS

ACKNOWLEDGEMENTS

To my dear husband—my Boaz—Walter Henderson III, or as I like to call him, Mr. Henderson.

Thank you for giving me the space needed to write without interruptions. Thank you for handling me delicately when I was so fragile. You are my royal king on earth and will always be my Boaz. I so appreciate you. Thank you for always allowing me to see Jesus in a man.

To my Berean Family Worship Center friends, colleagues, church ministry family, and Living By Precepts Ministries Advisory Board, thank you for being the blessings that you are. The Lord has given me the privilege to travel the world to share the Good News of Jesus Christ. I have been to many places and met lots of people, but I have never found or seen any like you. You have continued to show our family the love that has helped make it so easy to call you our mothers, spiritual sons, daughters, and friends. You are family to us. Thank you for continuing to show us Jesus in all your interactions.

To my ten living siblings, thank you for being my brothers and sisters. I could have been born in some other family and at some other time—if the truth be told, this was often my heart's desire. But when I look back over my life, through the ups and downs, the heated disagreements, the up close and personal conversations, and the times of intense fellowship, I would not trade any of you for another. Thank you for loving me when I felt unlovable. Thank you for correcting me when I didn't want to hear your corrections. Thank you for encouraging me when I so desperately needed to know I was loved unconditionally.

To my sister Shirley and my brother-in-love Casey, thank you for allowing me to stay in your home when I had no other place to lay my head and rest. I will never forget all you have done for me, and I will always honor you for the kindness you have shown me.

To our five living children: Nichole, Angela, Anntoinette Marie, Matthew, and Tremaine, I thank my God daily for each of you. What an absolute honor and privilege to be able to call you my son and daughters. "I have no greater joy than to hear that my children walk in truth" (3 John v. 4 KJV). When I see all the Lord has done and continues to do in and through your lives, my heart rejoices knowing that God is on our side, and we will not be moved. "I have set the Lord always before me: because he is at my right hand, I shall not be moved" (Psalm 16:8 KJV).

So, I take every opportunity to thank my God. He is the cloud by day and fire by night. Just as He went before the Israelites, He has walked me through fire, and I don't even smell like smoke. "And the Lord went before them by day in a pillar of a cloud, to lead them the way; and by night in a pillar of fire, to give them light; to go by day and night" (Exodus 13:21 KJV).

As the book of Isaiah says to you and me,

> "When you go through deep waters,
> I will be with you.
> When you go through rivers of difficulty,

you will not drown.
When you walk through the fire of oppression,
you will not be burned up;
the flames will not consume you."
(Isaiah 43:2 NLT)

Thank You, Lord.

INTRODUCTION

To understand the theme of this book, we must ask, "What is a **path**?" The dictionary tells us that a **path** is a way, or a track laid down for walking or traveling, created by continual and persistent treading in a certain direction to reach a desired destination. Let me put it in everyday vernacular—a **path** is a road so familiar, or one taken so many times, that you could even walk it blindfolded because you know every bump, rut, and landmark. You will not miss one twist or turn and will safely reach your desired destination.

FOUNDATION

As believers, we want to be on the right **path**. The Bible is very clear and even tells us to build our lives on a firm foundation—God's holy Word. I insist that all the teaching within these pages be biblically sound. So, let's take the time to dig into His Word and see what the Bible says about a **path**.

"Teach me, O Lord, the way of thy statutes; and I shall keep it unto the end. Give me understanding, and I shall keep thy law; Yea, I shall observe it with my whole heart. Make me to go in the **path** of thy commandments; for therein do I delight" (Psalm 119:33–35 KJV, author's emphasis).

"Thy word is a lamp unto my feet, and a light unto my **path**" (Psalm 119:105 KJV, author's emphasis).

"Give careful thought to the **paths** for your feet / and be steadfast in all your ways" (Proverbs 4:26 NIV, author's emphasis).

"Show me your ways, LORD, / teach me your **paths**" (Psalm 25:4 NIV, author's emphasis).

"Then you will understand what is right and just / and fair— every good **path**" (Proverbs 2:9 NIV, author's emphasis).

I'm offering every reader an invitation to de-wax their spiritual ears. Come on! It's time to lean in close as the Lord whispers and uncovers our steps to walking in the **path** God has for us. He is making us *A Planted Tree, Creating His* **Path** *to Freedom.*

ACRONYMS

Acronyms can be a particularly useful learning tool when you need to recall a list of items, remember crucial details, or drive home a critical point. So, I wanted to start my book by using the acronym **PATH** to help you remember and gain a deeper understanding of the importance of a spiritual **path**.

PATH

P:　　　**Praying** and **Persevering** lead to divine **Purpose.**

A:　　　**Anchored Ambassadors** lead to spiritual **Alignment.**

T:　　　**Timeless Truths** lead to complete **Transformation.**

H:　　　**Humility** and **Holiness** lead to inner **Healing.**

What can we learn from this acronym?

P: If you are faithful to *pray* and *persevere*, you will go down a **PATH** that will lead you to the **PURPOSE** God has for you.

A: If you surround yourself with *anchored ambassadors* of Christ, you will go down a **PATH** that leads to spiritual **ALIGNMENT**.

T: If you build your life on the *timeless truths* of God's Word, you will go down a **PATH** that will lead to **TRANSFORMATION**.

H: If you *humble* yourself and live a life of *holiness* before the Lord, He always pours out His grace, and you will go down a **PATH** that leads to inner **HEALING**.

Along every **path**, you will see signposts. These signposts are like heaven's "Amen Corner." So, you need your spiritual eyes and your spiritual ears to be open. Take time to study the signs along the **path** that the Lord has you on. You will soon discover His **path** is leading you to either your purpose, your transformation, or your inner healing. I will be sharing more about this at the end of each chapter.

THE SEED

Early one Tuesday morning, around the 2:00 a.m. watch, the seed for this manuscript was conceived in the womb of the birthing chamber of my heart. I received this clarion call to arms while I was lying there with my soul wide open to the Lord. He spoke in an almost audible voice, "Attention! I have destined your life experiences as a blueprint for others to walk in freedom."

I remembered Paul's admonition to the church at Corinth when he said, "Follow my example, as I follow the example of Christ" (1 Corinthians 11:1 NIV).

In the natural, not knowing the totality of what I had heard, all my adrenal glands kicked into full force. Beads of sweat formed across my forehead, and I scribbled down the thoughts and ideas that heaven was downloading to my soul. I felt compelled with an urgency to voice activate more of my life's untold story during this divine encounter. I allowed the Lord to surgically peel away any concealed layers of my life. There were many years of hidden secrets, shame, silence, and self-blame that I had tucked away in the deep recesses of my soul, and there were scars that I hid so no one could see or know. The evil tormentor constantly whispered that I would never measure up. The enemy continually taunted me for most of my formative years. So many painful memories of a cat-eyed, raggedy, toothless, sandy-red-haired little girl who was repeatedly tortured behind the wood heater opening in the shared bedroom began to play like a movie in my mind.

The Bible clearly speaks about what Satan has come for. As Jesus said, "The thief cometh not, but for to steal, and to kill, and to destroy: I am come that they might have life, and that they might have it more abundantly" (John 10:10 KJV).

I shouted a laundry list of crippling fears to the Lord: "I thought I had dealt with all this pain when I wrote my book—*Forgiving*

God's Way. I thought being married to the kindest and most godly Prince Charming on this side of heaven was proof that those deep wounds had been completely healed." My husband is a gift from God and has helped me walk through all kinds of trauma and pain.

However, no matter how hard I tried, I could not ignore or shake the voice of God thundering in my soul. He called me to draft this book. After a few minutes, I obeyed, and I am writing this mandate from God with a genuinely vulnerable spirit. I pray that every word will be a brick for you to plant your feet on and lead you farther down the **path** where freedom in Christ waits for you. I believe God is asking us to remove any superficial makeup that tries to cover up our scars. After all, Jesus is our example. He never hid His scars, so why should we? In fact, His scars are the only thing made by man in heaven. They serve as a reminder of the victory He won for each one of us.

There will be days we might limp down the **path**, but that's okay. Believers who have truly encountered the Lord walk with a limp and not a strut. Do you remember when Jacob wrestled with God? He was serious and needed God to bless him, and God did just that. This kind of limp isn't a sign of weakness; it's a sign of God's touch on a life. This is living proof that we can have victory on this side of heaven and not allow the enemy and past pain to dictate our destiny. For a patriarch of our faith, this is a limp of victory; Jacob had been forever changed by God. Scripture paints a beautiful picture of this moment when it says, "The sun rose above him as he passed Peniel, and he was limping because of his hip" (Genesis 32:31 NIV).

I have discovered this truth in my own life. No matter how challenging our **path** may be, there is a freedom and liberty we can have in Christ. We never have to live with a victim mindset because when we belong to Jesus, He makes us more than conquerors. "Nay, in all these things we are more than conquerors through him that loved us" (Romans 8:37 KJV). He makes all things work together for our good—and *all* means *all* (Romans 8:28, author's paraphrase).

I declare freedom over your life and future today. It is not by accident that you are reading these words right now. It is a divine appointment. You were born to be free and walk in the abundant life Christ has for you. As Jesus said, "If the Son therefore shall make you free, ye shall be free indeed" (John 8:36 KJV).

So, come on in and grab a seat. Let us pull up our mature bootstraps as we obtain the tools we will need to walk in victory from past pain. I must warn you, though—this is going to be straight talk from God's Word. If you don't like line upon line and precept upon precept teaching, you might want to put this book down before you start.

CAN'T PRAISE HIM ENOUGH

As the Lord leads, I will use every opportunity for praise breaks. I have to take them quite often because even after all these years of loving and serving Him, I remain in awe of His goodness and faithfulness that He continues to show me.

MEET MY GRANDMOTHERS —MY ANNIES

I always find very pleasant and delightful **paths** to walk through when I reminisce about my grandmothers. In my eyes, they could do nothing wrong. Both my grandmothers shared the same first name: Annie. They were very godly women and loved me well. I always felt special and safe in their presence. Although I was very private and never told them about the hidden abuse I endured, I believe they both knew in their hearts that I needed to be protected.

MAMA

I feel very honored to speak about my maternal grandmother Annie Mae, or as I called her, MaMa. This exceedingly rare jewel was such an inspiration in my life and in the lives of everyone who had the privilege of knowing her. To reach MaMa's home from my shanty shack at the depot, I had to walk several **paths**. They were well-worn because they had been heavily traveled.

However, even in the dark with my eyes closed or blindfolded, I would have arrived safely at MaMa's back door. It didn't matter if I was reading or writing; my little bare feet would trot straight to MaMa's house. They knew exactly how to get there.

The familiar smells that wafted through MaMa's home are still very fresh in my mind and evoke nostalgia after all these many years. I remember the big red sausages she pan-fried and served only to Grandfather Boykin, who I called Daddy. Those sausages were cooked in too much lard, but they always seemed to taste better when I stole one from Daddy's plate. Daddy was blind and I figured since he couldn't see, then he didn't know how many sausage pieces were on his plate. What could it hurt? But it never failed. Daddy would say, "Put it right back!" It was like he could see me stealing from his plate. I still don't know how he did that.

As I just told you, MaMa's house was always filled with distinct and enticing aromas of good food wafting through the house. Some of my favorite memories are the baked green apples or sweet potatoes in the oven with cinnamon on top. And I'll never forget her big chocolate cake that she cooked entirely too fast in a hot oven. It looked done on the outside, but it was raw in the middle. She boiled eggs the same way—the yolks were never hardened. I think you get the picture. The doughy middle and runny egg yolks didn't seem to matter. I loved the days I spent with MaMa. Oh, how I treasured those days skipping down those worn **paths** to get to her home. It was a haven for my young soul.

UNIVERSITY OF ADVERSITY

As a child, I was told MaMa only had an eighth-grade education, but now I realize she had graduated as a valedictorian from the University of Adversity. Whatever she went through in life made her seek the Lord and filled her with God's wisdom. MaMa walked deeply with the Lord, and I knew it. Her spiritual experience escalated her to the status of Chief Prayer Intercessor. When MaMa prayed, heaven paid attention, and I knew it. She had a hotline to the throne room. There were times I trembled when I heard her pray. MaMa's faith wasn't complicated. It was very simple, even childlike, but authentic to the core. God was her best friend, and she believed He would hear and answer her prayers. And guess what? I'm an eyewitness to the fact that God did hear and answer MaMa's prayers.

There was a time when MaMa was making preparation for dinner. However, the refrigerator was bare of the needed ingredients. This was one of those visible times when I saw MaMa kneeling in the kitchen to pray. There wasn't a long or even fancy prayer, but the power these words carried were very weighty. The prayer went simply, "Now Lord, I need food to be able to prepare dinner for us, and I trust You will send the answer from heaven. Amen!" Well, her prayer sure rose up to God, even as Cornelius's prayers did in Acts 10:31. There was a knock at the door, and groceries were brought and given to MaMa just in time to prepare the dinner meal. MaMa's faith and prayers were real and genuine, and God honored that. I am forever so very blessed to see that the University of Adversity could lead a woman to such true faith and reliance on God for provisions!

PRAISE BREAK

Right now, I have to stop and take a praise break. I certainly want to thank Him for giving me a wonderful grandmother like MaMa. Maybe you have someone in your life who has prayed for you and poured love into your life. Let's take a minute to thank the Lord for them.

PRAYER JOURNAL

Each chapter of *A Planted Tree: Creating His **PATH** to Freedom* will have a Prayer Journal section. Please use these parts of the book to slow down and soak up God's Word. You may want to have a journal alongside you for these sections or just write in the margins of your book. Whichever option you choose, know this is a time to connect with your Lord in a personal way. When you see the words "my," "me," or "I," replace them with your name. I have underlined some of the spots where you can fill in your own name. I think this will make the promises of God come alive to you.

Now let's circle back to what I shared with you about MaMa and prayer! Take time to look into God's Word and see what the Bible has to say about prayer. I think it will be a blessing to you.

"In the morning, Lord, you hear <u>my</u> voice; / in the morning <u>I</u> lay my requests before you / and wait expectantly" (Psalm 5:3 NIV, author's emphasis).

"Hear <u>my</u> cry, O God; Attend unto <u>my</u> prayer" (Psalm 61:1 KJV, author's emphasis).

"Hear <u>my</u> prayer, O God; Give ear to the words of <u>my</u> mouth" (Psalm 54:2 KJV, author's emphasis).

"<u>I</u> love the Lord, Because he hath heard <u>my</u> voice and <u>my</u> supplications. Because he hath inclined his ear unto <u>me</u>, Therefore will <u>I</u> call upon him as long as <u>I</u> live" (Psalm 116:1–2 KJV, author's emphasis).

"For my love they are my adversaries: but <u>I</u> give myself unto prayer" (Psalm 109:4 KJV, author's emphasis).

A FAITH LIKE HERS

These Scriptures are a few samples of the benefits of God's promises that MaMa believed and freely shared. Oh, how I wanted a faith like hers. My heart ached to believe God like she did. As a child, I could see that MaMa's confidence and faith in her heavenly Father made all our lives better. I hoped when I grew up, I would live as close to the Lord as MaMa did.

MaMa was queen of teachable moments. She found ways to shape my small soul for Jesus. One of the main things she pointed out to me was how much power there is in prayer. Now that I'm older, I realize she knew life could be cruel, and I would need to know how to reach out to the Lord. She encouraged me to pray even though I was young. At that time in my life, I didn't want prayer; I wanted revenge! I wanted the abuse to stop. I wanted someone to love me unconditionally. I was immature and couldn't see the benefits of praying, but I loved MaMa and would do whatever she asked. So, when she encouraged me to pray, I prayed.

But when I unfolded my hands and opened my eyes, the hurt was still there. My circumstances hadn't changed. Hopelessness and fear dominated my thinking. How could I tell MaMa what was going on? Would she even believe me? What would happen to my abusers? Although so much abuse was happening and sometimes I thought about a way to get even, I couldn't bear the thought of bad things happening to my abusers. So, I never told MaMa. I believed I was protecting her heart. I didn't want her to worry about me. I buried my hidden secret deep in the depths of my soul.

Another thing I loved about MaMa was that she always seemed to know what to say, how to say it, and when to say it. I can recount very vividly one heart-to-heart conversation we had together. MaMa said, "One day you're going to preach the gospel and feed hungry children in Africa."

Every time I heard MaMa speak those words, the enemy of my soul would whisper lies in the depths of my soul: "God can't use someone like you."

I knew MaMa couldn't be hearing correctly from the Lord. Deep inside my shattered heart, I was hoping to escape any more painful abuse, so I silently dreamed about an imaginary trip to Africa. Ironically, not knowing where Africa was on the map, I believed it would be a better place for me to be than behind the wood heater opening in the shared bedroom. So, I held on tightly to MaMa's words of prophesy.

HER WORDS CAME TO PASS

Fast forward to Port Elizabeth, South Africa, in 2001. My knees knocked together loudly. They sounded like a little drummer girl beating her drum, but after my initial stage fright, God poured iron into my spine. He gave me courage and confidence to stand before a large group of people and proclaim God's Word.

A few years after my second trip back to South Africa, I had the distinct honor of feeding many hungry children as they lined up for a bowl of soup. MaMa's prophecy, so many decades before, came to pass. Tears of gratitude still run down my cheeks whenever I think about this.

When it didn't seem like God was working or even cared, He was, and He did. He never stopped working, and He never stopped caring about me. Thank you, MaMa, for speaking life over me. Thank you for being God's prophetess and His instrument of healing. My life was changed forever because of your love and prayers. Thank you for allowing God to use you as His mouthpiece.

PRAISE BREAK

Looking back, I can see how God's hand of mercy carried me all my life. Right now, I have to stop and take another praise break and thank the Lord for His faithfulness. Why don't you take a moment to remember the times He has been faithful to you. Take this time to thank Him.

CLAIM HIS PROMISES

The Bible is filled with promises that God has made to His people. Whether these promises were spoken through prophets recorded in the Old Testament Scriptures or apostles in the New Testament Word, *you* can claim His promises today too. When you and I are walking in obedience to God's will, His promises are there for us too.

"Being confident of this very thing, that he which hath begun a good work in you will perform it until the day of Jesus Christ" (Philippians 1:6 KJV).

"But forget all that—
it is nothing compared to what I am going to do.
For I am about to do something new.
See, I have already begun! Do you not see it?
I will make a **pathway** through the wilderness.
I will create rivers in the dry wasteland."
(Isaiah 43:18–19 NLT, author's emphasis)

"And I will bring the blind by a way that they knew not; I will lead them in **paths** that they have not known: I will make darkness light before them, and crooked things straight. These things will I do unto them, and not forsake them" (Isaiah 42:16 KJV).

Through God's Word, I've come to understand this truth: The past doesn't dictate my future, and it doesn't have to dictate yours either. It cannot define or bind us because once God's mercy finds us, we are free! God measures all things by His hands and creates His **path** to freedom. Don't believe the lies of Satan; he will tell you there is no hope for you and your life will never change. It's not true. Your heavenly Father is offering you complete freedom. Follow that **path** and leave your chains behind.

MA-MISSY

As a young child, I was captivated by the outward beauty of my paternal grandmother Annie Laura, who I called Ma-Missy. Her outward beauty, shiny sandy hair, hazel eyes, and hourglass figure always attracted attention even if she did not want it or welcome it. When Ma-Missy walked into a room, even the blind man's eyes blinked and desired to open. Her gorgeous face, perfect physique, and charming ways were not the only things beautiful about Ma-Missy. She was just as beautiful on the inside as she was on the outside. Her heart was huge. She always made sure I had enough food to eat and clothes to wear. But she wasn't only generous to me; she gave to anyone in need. God had blessed her with a gift of hospitality and generosity. She had a merciful spirit and refused to be self-righteous or judgmental. She believed it pleased the Lord to love people.

> "Is it not to share your food with the hungry
> and to provide the poor wanderer with shelter—
> when you see the naked, to clothe them,
> and not to turn away from your own flesh and blood?"
> (Isaiah 58:7 NIV)

When I walked in Ma-Missy's home, it smelled like her delicious teacakes. Back then, I did not realize this delectable snack was a delicacy for dignitaries. I was privileged to eat as many as my belly could hold. Before I left, without fail, Ma-Missy would allow me to place at least two teacakes in a napkin and roll them up in my frayed shirt or tuck them into my bag to eat later. Oh, how I wish I could eat at least two of Ma-Missy's teacakes right now. And knowing Ma-Missy, she would insist I share some with you.

Ma-Missy, thank you for never judging me for others' or my mistakes. Thank you for always loving me unconditionally. Thank you for showing me how to serve and love others well. Thank you for being my exquisite and elegant grandmother. Thank you for always showing me Jesus and giving me a godly foundation and legacy to build on.

Remembering how I saw Jesus in my dear Ma-Missy, I am reminded of a verse from John: "The same came therefore to Philip, which was of Bethsaida of Galilee, and him, saying, Sir, we would see Jesus" (John 12:21 KJV).

Paul spoke of the faithful women in Timothy's life so beautifully when he said, "I remember your genuine faith, for you share the faith that first filled your grandmother Lois and your mother, Eunice. And I know that same faith continues strong in you" (2 Timothy 1:5 NLT). MaMa and Ma-Missy were the faithful women who left me with this same legacy.

GRANDMA'S TRANSLATION

Sometimes people may ask me what translation of the Bible I like the best. I have come to the conclusion that although I enjoy studying various versions of God's Word, I like my grandmothers' translations the best. They gave me a sample, an actual *living example,* of what true Christianity looks like. They left behind large footprints, and they are easy for me to find. They were like mighty oak trees in my life. They weathered so many storms and never lost their faith. I continue to cherish both of my Annies.

Their prayer life, love for God's Word, integrity, unconditional love, generosity, hospitality, support, and godly character gave me a firm foundation to build my life on and created plain and straight **paths** that I continue to walk in still today.

SIGNPOST

Remember how I shared in the Introduction about the signposts along the way? Let's take a minute to look and see if we can find one. Which letter in the acronym do you think best fits the influence my godly grandmothers had on me?

I feel like the impact they had on my life could be found in every letter, but I am going to choose the letter A. When I was with MaMa or Ma-Missy, I was surrounded by *anchored ambassadors* for Jesus, and they represented Him well. If you are surrounded by *anchored ambassadors* for Jesus and let them speak into your life, you will go down a **PATH** that leads to proper spiritual **ALIGNMENT**.

Please keep in mind that the Holy Spirit speaks to each of God's children in unique ways. As you read through each chapter, you may see a different letter from the acronym that jumps out! That is just fine. These Signpost sections are here to pull your mind back into focusing on the **path** that God has for you, not to getting the *right answer*.

Chapter 2

MY PARENTS

There have been others who have helped in creating a **path** for me to travel down. Two of the most important were my father, Mr. Timothy, and my mother, Mrs. Catherine. I do not know where I would be without their influence. I will be forever grateful for the way they taught me life lessons. They both instilled a strong, tremendous work ethic in my siblings and me. I never would have made it without their example. They set the bar high for all of their children. I thank God for choosing them to be my parents. The older I get, the more I appreciate the way they kept clothes on my back, food in my belly, and the home fires burning. They provided a shelter from many storms of life. I can't help but honor them. Their lives testify from the grave of the goodness of God. I am looking forward to the family reunion we will have one day in heaven. Though they are gone, the faith they found during their life journey still speaks for them.

The fact that my parents' life and faith journey *still speaks for them* connects to another verse from Scripture. "Because Abel had faith, he offered God a better sacrifice than Cain did. God was pleased with him and his gift, and even though Abel is now dead, his faith still speaks for him" (Hebrews 11:4 CEV).

If you are a parent, I know the days can seem long, but I assure you the years are short. I encourage you to keep showing up for your children. Be there. Be available. Be their *anchored ambassador* for Jesus. You are doing holy work. They won't ever forget you and your care. You will never regret the time you invested in them. This will be the most important investment you will ever make— far more important than an impressive financial portfolio.

Many times, we get it all backwards. We think to raise children we need a fancy house or expensive car. I realize those things can be convenient and make life a little easier, but I've found that the people who left footprints in my soul are the ones who loved Jesus with all their hearts and kept on showing up.

The impact of loving Christian parents can be profound and far-reaching. You might be asking, "What are the key areas where my influence can be especially powerful?" Here is a short list for you.

✓ **Spiritual Foundation**
Godly parents can provide children with a solid foundation to build their lives on. This keeps them grounded throughout all the difficulties of life.

✓ **Moral Compass**
Through your example, your children can learn the importance of integrity, kindness, humility, and God's love. Parents who live out their faith daily show their children the importance of

righteous living, and this builds strong moral character. Remember it's like that old saying: Children learn more from what is "caught" than what is "taught."

- ✓ **Sense of Identity**
  When children have parents who aren't ashamed of their faith and speak life to them, it gives them a deep and clear sense of identity. This instills in them a deep confidence in God to face the world.

Are you seeing the pattern here? A committed Christian mother or father provides a **path** for their children. And even if some children might rebel, the spiritual foundation instilled in them often brings them back to the values and truths they were taught.

SIGNPOST

Can you find the signpost along this **path**? Which letter in the acronym do you think best fits the influence of my parents? Once again, I feel like the impact they had on my life could be found in every letter. They were *anchored ambassadors* for Christ, but looking back, the thing that stands out to me is knowing my parents provided for me, prayed for me, and persevered through whatever life threw at them. So, I am going to choose the letter P. If you have someone providing, praying, and persevering for the Lord, you have been given a tremendous gift. Watch how their prayers lead you down a **PATH** of **PURPOSE**. I've come to know prayer never fails to produce God's expected end.

PRAISE BREAK

I need to take another praise break and thank the Lord for all the ways He has had His hand on my life. When I look back, I see His fingerprints all over the place. Hallelujah! Take this time to thank the Lord for the people who have provided, prayed, and persevered for you.

PRAYER JOURNAL

You have reached your second chance to slow down and soak in God's Word. Take out your journal, pen, or highlighter and make time to be still with the Lord. Reflect back on the power that parents and mentors can have in a child's life and soak up these verses.

"And thou shalt teach them diligently unto thy children, and shalt talk of them when thou sittest in thine house, and when thou walkest by the way, and when thou liest down, and when thou risest up. And thou shalt bind them for a sign upon thine hand, and they shall be as frontlets between thine eyes" (Deuteronomy 6:7–8 KJV).

"In thee, O LORD, do I put my trust; let me never be ashamed: deliver me in thy righteousness" (Psalm 31:1 KJV).

"Evil people will surely be punished, / but the children of the godly will go free" (Proverbs 11:21 NLT).

"Direct your children onto the right **path**, / and when they are older, they will not leave it" (Proverbs 22:6 NLT, author's emphasis).

"I have no greater joy than to hear that my children walk in truth" (3 John v. 4 KJV).

As you finish your prayer time, answer this question—has the Lord sent you down a **path** that calls you to guard and watch over dear children? It is a high calling if He has.

The **PATH** the Lord has led me down has led me to my divine **PURPOSE**. He called me into the ministry, and His will has taken me around the globe. I often stand in awe of the tremendous privileges God has given me to speak before small, medium, and large crowds of people. I praise the Lord for the **path** I am on. So, I never will despise small beginnings. Just as it says in Zechariah, "Do not despise these small beginnings, for the Lord rejoices to see the work begin" (Zechariah 4:10 NLT).

MY JOURNALS

As I pondered over how to piece this story together, the Lord reminded me of my cherished collection of journals. I have at least fifty-two finished journals full of hidden treasures. Each one has a story of its own—some with straight and others with crooked **paths** of training, but all so dear. I have penned many short stories and written glimpses of the **paths** the Lord has led me down. Whenever I open one of my journals and reread just how faithful and good God has been, I have to stop and brush the tears from my eyes and take a praise break. God has always been and continues to be faithful to His Word and to me, even on days I am weak and have moments of doubt. Just as Paul said to Timothy, "If we are unfaithful, / he remains faithful, / for he cannot deny who he is" (2 Timothy 2:13 NLT).

My journals are not diaries. A diary is about things we've done, but a journal is about the lessons we've learned along the way. This distinction is similar to the difference between knowledge and wisdom. We can take the time to document the **paths** we've walked, the many mistakes we've made, and how God always brought us through to victory!

In the first chapter of this book, I encourage you to *claim His promises*. Think of claiming a promise as you read this excerpt from Isaiah:

> "When you pass through the waters, I will be with you;
> And through the rivers, they will not overwhelm you.
> When you walk through fire, you will not be scorched,
> Nor will the flame burn you."
> (Isaiah 43:2 AMP)

What a promise from God! We can go through fires and not even smell like the smoke we've come through. Do you remember the story of the three Hebrew boys Shadrach, Meshach, and Abednego? They were thrown in a fiery furnace. They didn't know how God was going to deliver them. They knew He could, but they said that even if He didn't, they would not serve the false gods.

"Shadrach, Meshach and Abednego replied to him, 'King Nebuchadnezzar, we do not need to defend ourselves before you in this matter. If we are thrown into the blazing furnace, the God we serve is able to deliver us from it, and he will deliver us from Your Majesty's hand. But even if he does not, we want you to know, Your Majesty, that we will not serve your gods or worship the image of gold you have set up'" (Daniel 3:16–18 NIV).

We all know the story. God did deliver them.

But maybe your experience is like mine—you had a painful and shameful past. God has given you some incredibly special promises. We have His Word on it. He has a miraculous way of writing glory in every story that is given to Him. Just as Joel said to the Israelites,

> The Lord says, "I will give you back what you lost
> to the swarming locusts, the hopping locusts,
> the stripping locusts, and the cutting locusts.
> It was I who sent this great destroying army against you."
> (Joel 2:25 NLT)

God never stops working behind the scenes on our behalf. He always has great victory in store. "And we know that all things work together for good to them that love God, to them who are the called according to his purpose" (Romans 8:28 KJV). But we have to remember that glory never looks like glory when it's on the way to us. Sometimes we can't see it through the tears. But God has power to make our midnight hour our finest hour. Faith always shines brightest in dark. The wounded Healer hasn't lost His touch. Remember how He took Saul of Tarsus, a persecutor of the church, and saved him and completely transformed him—even changed his name to Paul. Out of twenty-seven books in the New Testament, thirteen or fourteen are traditionally attributed to Paul. God put him on a **path**—it was a street called Straight and Narrow. God has a **path** for you too.

PATH OF FREEDOM THROUGH THE STORMS

And that's why I believe the Lord is having me share portions of my stories that I've recorded in my journals with you all. I pray this might help you become *A Planted Tree, Creating His **Path** to Freedom*. I never want to bring shame to the gospel or dishonor anyone in my past, present, or future. The same God who gave me freedom wants to give others freedom. "He comforts us in all our troubles so that we can comfort others. When they are troubled, we will be able to give them the same comfort God has given us" (2 Corinthians 1:4 NLT).

The life I've lived has taught me that some storms the Lord allowed came to clear my **path**. While my childhood was filled with storms that threatened to break me, I was held strong by the roots that had been set in rich soil. My parents made mistakes, as all men and women do, but where they fell short, my grandmothers came in. God knew the **path** my life would take, and He continues to make new ways for me to this day. So, my future is bright and yours can be too. And the Lord made it truly clear that He is no respecter of persons. In other words, He is not partial to those with wealth or status, and He does not show favoritism. Christians from the early church saw this truth too, and this point is shown in the book of Acts: "Then Peter began to speak: 'I now realize how true it is that God does not show favoritism'" (Acts 10:34 NIV).

What He has done for me, He can do for you. So, lean in closer as we begin to uncover some very rare jewels.

A PLANTED TREE

Oh, the joys of those who do not
follow the advice of the wicked,
or stand around with sinners,
or join in with mockers.
But they delight in the law of the LORD,
meditating on it day and night.
They are like trees planted along the riverbank,
bearing fruit each season.
Their leaves never wither,
and they prosper in all they do.

But not the wicked!
They are like worthless chaff, scattered by the wind.
They will be condemned at the time of judgment.
Sinners will have no place among the godly.
For the LORD watches over the **path** of the godly,
but the **path** of the wicked leads to destruction.
(Psalm 1:1–6 NLT, author's emphasis)

WHAT IS A TREE?

The dictionary says a tree is "a plant having a permanent woody main stem or trunk, ordinarily growing to a considerable height, and usually developing branches at some distance from the ground."[1]

Trees also have roots that go down very deep into the ground. If you look this up for yourself, you will see that, depending on the type of tree, roots may reach three to seven feet into the soil! To remove the average tree, you cannot just yank it up with your hand. You have to hire a tree removal professional (arborist) to dig it up from the root. What you see on the surface is not the whole tree . . . far from it. There is a reason that roots must go down so deep into the ground.

Look back up at the verses from Psalm 1 above. Why do you think I titled this chapter "A Planted Tree"? The roots of a tree serve the same purpose that God often does for His children. Seasons come and seasons go. The storm comes, the wind blows, the hot sun beats down on the tree, the snow covers the tree branches, and the bitter cold in winter causes its leaves to turn brown and finally bare. But because every tree has a root system from which it draws life and nourishment, when springtime comes, we can see the buds begin to sprout again. The leaves begin to spread their arms as they bounce back and bear their fruit on the vine at the right time of the year. While a tree's roots allow it to weather storms and harsh winters, God allows His people to weather life's

---

1   *Dictionary.com,* s.v. "tree (*n.*)," accessed February 10, 2025, https://www.dictionary.com/browse/tree.

trials. Let's look at another metaphor from nature that comes up in the Word.

THE VINE AND THE BRANCHES

Jesus spoke about vines because the metaphors made sense to the farming communities that were so common centuries ago. I am trying to show, with *A Planted Tree: Creating His **PATH** to Freedom*, that we all need to think a bit more about our Christian roots and where we get our life from! In apple orchards we see Red Delicious, Granny Smith, Pink Lady, Gala, Honeycrisp, and many more varieties (by the way, these are all types of my husband's favorite apples). Just as those beautiful apple trees provide delicious fruit, our lives can produce sweetness . . . when we are connected to God! In similar manner, we will bear much fruit when we stay connected to the Vine that gives the right nourishment. Jesus said this so beautifully in John's Gospel: "Yes, I am the vine; you are the branches. Those who remain in me, and I in them, will produce much fruit. For apart from me you can do nothing" (John 15:5 NLT).

Who is the Vine? What is the correct nourishment for us? I'm glad you asked. There is only one place to find the answer—God's Word. All the promises of God to every believer are yes and amen!

"Whatever God has promised gets stamped with the Yes of Jesus. In him, this is what we preach and pray, the great Amen, God's Yes and our Yes together, gloriously evident. God affirms us, making us a sure thing in Christ, putting his Yes within us. By his Spirit he has stamped us with his eternal pledge—a sure beginning of what he is destined to complete" (2 Corinthians 1:20 MSG).

God is the Promise Keeper. There might be others who have broken their vows to us, but God is not like that. He keeps His promises. He cannot and will not ever lie. When you and I are planted and grounded in Him, every chapter, every verse, every line, and all of His promises are true. We can have trust in His Word! Why? God is the Word and the Word is God. For just as it says in John, "In the beginning was the Word, and the Word was with God, and the Word was God" (John 1:1 KJV).

PRAISE BREAK

I have to take another praise break. When I remember the faithfulness of the Lord, I can't help but raise my hands, open my mouth, and praise Him. For those who don't understand my deep devotion, I can only tell you this—my worship is for real. If you don't understand my past pain, you'll never understand my present praise. I often feel like the forgiven woman who broke a beautiful alabaster jar filled with expensive perfume and poured it on the feet of Jesus in a holy act of worship. As her tears of thankfulness flowed, she was criticized, but Jesus welcomed and received her praise. Never be ashamed to worship the One who died for you. This isn't one of our Prayer Journal spots, but I do want you to read through this account from Luke's Gospel:

> One of the Pharisees asked Jesus to have dinner
> with him, so Jesus went to his home and sat down
> to eat. When a certain immoral woman from
> that city heard he was eating there, she brought

a beautiful alabaster jar filled with expensive perfume. Then she knelt behind him at his feet, weeping. Her tears fell on his feet, and she wiped them off with her hair. Then she kept kissing his feet and putting perfume on them. When the Pharisee who had invited him saw this, he said to himself, "If this man were a prophet, he would know what kind of woman is touching him. She's a sinner!" (Luke 7:36–47 NLT)

GOD'S WORD IS ALIVE AND POWERFUL

Sometimes people will ask, "Do you believe God's Word is alive?" I absolutely do, but don't take my word for it. The Bible makes it very clear. "God's word is alive and powerful! It is sharper than any double-edged sword. His word can cut through our spirits and souls and through our joints and marrow, until it discovers the desires and thoughts of our hearts" (Hebrews 4:12 CEV).

GOD'S WORD IS TRUTH

When we're walking in the midst of pain, at times all we want is revenge and an end to the pain or trauma. This is a great time to roll all our burdens and cares over on the Lord. WHY? I am confident, just like Moses was when he was speaking to Joshua and the children of Israel. He told Joshua that he had to be strong and courageous, and he reminded Joshua that the Lord would go with him—even before him (Deuteronomy 31:8, author's paraphrase). I am persuaded that I don't have to be afraid or discouraged, for the Lord will personally go ahead of me! He will be with me; He will neither fail me nor abandon me. I have His word on this!

PRAYER JOURNAL

It is time, again, to slow down and meditate on verses that will pull you back to this chapter's main message. When you focus on being *A Planted Tree* in God's kingdom, you will need to lean into the truth found in God's Word. So, take out your journal, pens, and highlighters and meditate on these next few verses I've picked out for you.

"Sanctify them by the truth; your word is truth" (John 17:17 NIV).

"Your word is a lamp to guide my feet and a light for my **path**" (Psalm 119:105 NLT, author's emphasis).

"For ever, O LORD, thy word is settled in heaven" (Psalm 119:89 KJV).

GOD'S WORD WORKS

When something doesn't work as promised, we often play the blame game. But most of the time we discover that it is the operator's error. We try to get it to work in a wrong or incorrect manner. That's exactly how it is with God's Word. We carelessly throw out Bible verses and don't dig deeper to the condition with the promise. There is always God's part and our part. So, let's come closer so we can understand how God's Word works. God gives us a promise in His Word. Then, faith believes the promise, hope anticipates the promise, and patience waits for the promise.

Since we know God is faithful, we can quietly and patiently wait until God fulfills His word.

OUR PART

What should our posture be as we wait on the Lord's promises? We should wait quietly.

"It is good that a man should both hope and **quietly** wait for the salvation of the Lord" (Lamentations 3:26 KJV, author's emphasis).

We should wait patiently.

> I **patiently** waited, LORD,
> for you to hear my prayer.
> You listened and pulled me
> from a lonely pit
> full of mud and mire.
> You let me stand on a rock
> with my feet firm,
> and you gave me a new song,
> a song of praise to you.
> Many will see this,
> and they will honor and trust
> you, the LORD God.
> (Psalm 40:1–3 CEV, author's emphasis)

BROKENNESS

Since we're talking about *our* part, let's first acknowledge that all of us are broken . . . at least in certain areas and times of our lives.

There are two distinct kinds of brokenness that define our journey as humans and believers. The first is a brokenness that stems from the pain and consequences of sin. It's the broken heart of loss, the wounded spirit crushed by betrayal, and the emptiness left by separation from God. This kind of brokenness is universal, affecting us all at some point in life. Yet, God desires to heal every fracture and mend every wound, restoring us through His grace and love. His healing transforms our pain into purpose, reminding us that no brokenness is beyond His reach.

The second kind of brokenness is a humility of heart that comes from surrendering fully to God. It's not the result of sin but of a willing spirit that yields to the Lord's refining work. This brokenness is beautiful, for it aligns us with God's will and allows Him to mold us into His image.

Like an unbroken horse that is strong but unsafe, a stubborn un-surrendered heart is untamed and unreliable. However, when a horse is broken, its strength and talent are channeled into something greater than itself. Similarly, when we allow God to break us in humility, our lives become a powerful testimony of His strength at work within us. It is through this surrender that our potential is fully realized, and we become instruments of His glory. An unbroken horse cannot be trusted, but neither can an unbroken believer.

GOD'S PART

We all have rejoiced when our loved ones get jobs that have benefits. We are excited for them and realize employment benefits can be a game changer. The same is true with spiritual benefits.

There are promises in the Bible that have benefits. Don't just take my word for it. Read this psalm of David for yourself: "Bless the LORD, O my soul, and forget not all his benefits" (Psalm 103:2 KJV).

You might be asking, "What are some benefits of God's promises?" Well, let's find out. There are parts of the book of Isaiah that speak of comfort for God's people: "But they that wait upon the LORD shall renew their strength; they shall mount up with wings as eagles; they shall run, and not be weary; and they shall walk, and not faint" (Isaiah 40:31 KJV). This verse from Isaiah promises rejuvenation from God. Note that this promise specifies "they that wait upon the LORD."

TRAVEL LIGHT SO YOU CAN COMMIT YOUR WAY TO THE LORD

Let's look at another one of God's promises. You just read a psalm that speaks of God's benefits for His people. Earlier in this chapter you read that *our part* involves waiting quietly and patiently. There is another psalm that speaks of something that God's people must do for Him: "Commit thy way unto the Lord; trust also in him; and he shall bring it to pass" (Psalm 37:5 KJV).

Another aspect of our part is to commit our way to the Lord. Life can be very heavy at times, but here is the good news—Jesus has broad shoulders, and He wants us to cast every cumbersome burden and care over to Him. And when we do, He doesn't want us to reel those worries back in. He wants us to leave them with Him so we can travel light through this life.

"Come to me, all you who are weary and burdened, and I will give you rest. Take my yoke upon you and learn from me, for I am gentle and humble in heart, and you will find rest for your souls" (Matthew 11:28–29 NIV).

Is there something troubling you right now? Let's pause and take a minute so that you can give it to the Lord. *Do your part.* Commit your way to the Lord, and He promises to work behind the scenes and bring such beautiful things to pass.

Is there anything that you're trying to walk away from that God might be asking you to stay and walk through? He will give you His strength to press into His **path** of righteousness. This course leads to great overcoming victory. As it says in Revelation, "And they overcame him by the blood of the Lamb and by the word of their testimony, and they did not love their lives to the death" (Revelation 12:11 NKJV).

DON'T GIVE UP

Right now, I speak this declaration over you. Don't give up on God. Hold on. He won't ever give up on you. If His Word states it, He will bring it to pass. Let's look at some more promises we can plant our feet and faith on. His Word is the one thing that's for certain in these uncertain times. It's the **path** we're pressing to be on.

Teach me, O LORD, the way of thy statutes; and
I shall keep it unto the end.

Give me understanding, and I shall keep thy law;
yea, I shall observe it with my whole heart.

Make me to go in the **path** of thy commandments;
for therein do I delight. (Psalm 119:33–35 KJV,
author's emphasis)

While these verses from Psalm 119 call out to God asking for guidance, Psalm 37 begins with David's call to revel in what God will provide when He is trusted! As he so beautifully wrote, "Take delight in the LORD, / and he will give you your heart's desires" (Psalm 37:4 NLT).

TIMELESS TRUTHS

Let us call some *timeless truths* to remembrance. God made us in His image, and He is the Author and Finisher of your story—it never ends in ashes. He always writes His glory in every story that is given to Him. You aren't a quitter! You're running to win and will finish strong! He has called you to become *A Planted Tree, Creating His* **Path** *to Freedom.*

Isaiah spoke *timeless truths* as well. He may have been calling the people of Judah and Jerusalem, but his words call out to you just as clearly! God anointed Isaiah "to appoint unto them that mourn in Zion, to give unto them beauty for ashes, the oil of joy for mourning, the garment of praise for the spirit of heaviness, that they might be called **trees** of righteousness, the planting of the Lord, that He might be glorified" (Isaiah 61:3 KJV, author's emphasis).

SIGNPOST

Let's stop and take a minute to look and see if we can find a signpost. Which letter in the acronym do you think best fits the influence and power God's Word has on you? The Bible has supernatural impartation, and faith comes when we read it. So, I am going to choose the letter T. When we get into God's Word, it gets into us, and we will go down a **PATH** that leads to complete **TRANSFORMATION**. Just as the soil's nutrients are pulled up through a tree's strong roots and a branch pulls life from the vine, we will be changed forever from our source, the Word!

Chapter 4

WARRING WITH GOD'S WORD

For many years I believed outward circumstances had the power to bring hope, joy, and peace. I thought all the accolades and awards would satisfy the ache I felt deep in my soul. I just knew by decorating the external walls of my home with plaques, diplomas, degrees, and certificates, they would numb and stop the internal hurt and pain that I could not get rid of no matter how hard I tried. But it didn't work!

I was blinded by unsanctified ambition. I tried almost anything and used anyone I believed would help me get what I wanted and where I wanted to be. I am embarrassed to admit that I had accepted the mentality and posture that I would use others first because I was not ever going to be abused, tormented, tortured, or victimized again.

THE UPSIDE-DOWN KINGDOM

I didn't realize the principles of God's kingdom yet. You see, His kingdom is an upside-down kingdom that's really a right-side-up kingdom. Are you following this? If you don't believe me, listen to these biblical principles:

If you want to be great, become a servant. (Try that on Wall Street.)

The last will be first. (Say what?)

The way up is down. (You mean to rise in this kingdom, you must humble yourself?)

Make the most of the least of these. (Wait! But the least of these cannot help you get ahead.)

I think you get the picture. This kingdom is a spiritual kingdom. We must be emptied of sin and self so there is only room for the King. It's so different from a worldly kingdom. As Paul said, "the kingdom of God is not eating and drinking, but righteousness and peace and joy in the Holy Spirit" (Romans 14:17 NKJV).

SPIRITUAL KNOTHOLES

Have you ever heard that a lot of people have to be pulled through a knothole to get straightened out? Unfortunately, pain is a master teacher. And I went through many disastrous, life-changing experiences trying to find my way. I was looking for hope, joy, and peace, but I had to learn that only Jesus could satisfy my soul. If we look outside of Him for answers, we will be greatly disappointed. I was searching in all the wrong places and spending too much time with the wrong people. Oh, but a kind King loved me too much to leave me in my deep despair. He came looking for me, and I'm so glad He did.

PARABLE OF THE SOWER

Throughout Jesus's parables, He often used imagery of planting with the purpose to communicate profound truths. In the parable of the sower, the seed of God's Word takes root and yields an abundant harvest only when planted in the good soil of a receptive heart.

> Again Jesus began to teach by the lake. The crowd that gathered around him was so large that he got into a boat and sat in it out on the lake, while all the people were along the shore at the water's edge. He taught them many things by parables, and in his teaching said: "Listen! A farmer went out to sow his seed. As he was scattering the seed, some fell along the **path**, and the birds came and ate it up. Some fell on rocky places, where it did not have much soil. It sprang up quickly, because the soil was shallow. But when the sun came up, the plants were scorched, and they withered because they had no root. Other seed fell among thorns, which grew up and choked the plants, so that they did not bear grain. Still other seed fell on good soil. It came up, grew and produced a crop, some multiplying thirty, some sixty, some a hundred times." (Mark 4:1–8 NIV, author's emphasis)

PARABLE OF THE VINE AND BRANCHES

Similarly, the parable of the vine and branches underscores the necessity of staying connected to Jesus, the true Vine, to produce lasting fruit.

"I am the true vine, and my Father is the gardener. He cuts off every branch in me that bears no fruit, while every branch that does bear fruit he prunes so that it will be even more fruitful. You are already clean because of the word I have spoken to you. Remain in me, as I also remain in you. No branch can bear fruit by itself; it must remain in the vine. Neither can you bear fruit unless you remain in me.

"I am the vine; you are the branches. If you remain in me and I in you, you will bear much fruit; apart from me you can do nothing. If you do not remain in me, you are like a branch that is thrown away and withers; such branches are picked up, thrown into the fire and burned. If you remain in me and my words remain in you, ask whatever you wish, and it will be done for you. This is to my Father's glory, that you bear much fruit, showing yourselves to be my disciples. . . .

"You did not choose me, but I chose you and appointed you so that you might go and bear fruit—fruit that will last—and so that whatever

you ask in my name the Father will give you."
(John 15:1–8, 16 NIV)

Together, these parables of the sower and the vine highlight the vital need for both spiritual growth and total reliance on Jesus. And look what God promises when we wholly follow the Lord in this way:

> He shall be like a tree
> Planted by the rivers of water,
> That brings forth its fruit in its season,
> Whose leaf also shall not wither;
> And whatever he does shall prosper.
> (Psalm 1:3 NKJV)

THE ABUNDANT LIFE

Let's take a few minutes to examine the benefits of following the Lord in a deeper way. How does a life full of hope, joy, and peace sound to you? If we do our part and have receptive hearts and receive His Word gladly, miracles happen in our souls. When we abide in the Vine, inner healings take place. We will no longer be the same. Oh, I pray as you read these words, you will be changed forever. Jesus wants to do this for you.

HOPE

How we need hope in these desperate days! What is hope? It's been described as a feeling of expectation and trust for a certain thing to happen. It's something that we do not ever want to live without. We have read about and seen what hopeless people do.

A very vivid memory comes to my mind. I was a young adult and didn't have the necessary items for physical survival, nor the mental capacity to move forward. I had lost all hope. So, I decided I would put God to the test. I wanted to see if He was just my grandmother's God or if I could trust Him to help me if I asked Him.

Where do you go when you've done everything humanly possible and you've spent your last penny? Who do you talk to when you can't sleep at night because crippling fears are taunting you? I sobbed. I pleaded. I prayed, "Where are You, God? Do You hear me? Do You even care?" When the silence was deafening and no one seemed to have an answer, I kept crying to the Lord, and He heard me right in the middle of my confusion and mess.

After hours of tossing and turning, I now know that I had allowed the enemy to fill my head with lies. "You're not going to get through this one! You're getting what you deserve for all you've done wrong! God doesn't hear you. Give up and take what you deserve!"

But, late in the midnight hour, I heard my God, my Savior, my Healer, my Deliverer's voice speak to my heart. He said, "Don't give up on Me, and I won't give up on you!"

So, when someone asks me where I put my hope, I always tell them, "My only hope is in Jesus." David's psalms, whether for music or not, fit so well into my own heart. He too said, "And so, Lord, where do I put my hope? / My only hope is in you" (Psalm 39:7 NLT).

The Bible is the best commentary of itself. We have a firm foundation to build our faith upon when we are seeking an abundant life. Do you remember what Jesus did when He was tempted by the devil in the wilderness? He quoted the Word of God to defeat the enemy. We can do the same.

After Jesus had fasted for forty days, Satan came to Him. "And when the tempter came to him, he said, If thou be the Son of God, command that these stones be made bread. But he answered and said, It is written, Man shall not live by bread alone, but by every word that proceedeth out of the mouth of God" (Matthew 4:3–4 KJV).

Let the fact that Jesus spoke Scripture back to Satan sink in. Then, move on down to the next section and speak the Word over your own life.

PRAYER JOURNAL

In this Prayer Journal section, I want you to use God's Word as a weapon, just as Jesus did. There is *power* in these words. Remember to put your name in the following Scriptures where you see the words "me," "my," or "you." Speak them over your life and what you are walking through right now.

David wrote these words when he was running from his own son: "Many are saying of <u>me</u>, There is no help for <u>him</u> in God. Selah [pause, and calmly think of that]! / But You, O Lord, are a shield for <u>me</u>, <u>my</u> glory, and the lifter of <u>my</u> head" (Psalm 3:2–3 AMPC, author's emphasis).

The conversation between the angel Gabriel and Mary is another amazing Scripture to speak over your life. "'For with God nothing [is or ever] shall be impossible.' Then Mary said, 'Behold, I am the servant of the Lord; may it be done to me according to your word'" (Luke 1:37–38 AMP, author's emphasis). May we all be willing as Mary was!

As Moses said, "Do not be afraid or discouraged, for the LORD will personally go ahead of you. He will be with you; he will neither fail you nor abandon you" (Deuteronomy 31:8 NLT, author's emphasis).

Speak words of hope over yourself through this psalm:

O Lord, you alone are my **hope**.
I've trusted you, O LORD, from childhood.
Yes, you have been with me from birth;
from my mother's womb you have cared for me.
No wonder I am always praising you!
(Psalm 71:5–6 NLT, author's emphasis)

Paul prayed, thousands of years ago, and said, "I pray that God, the source of **hope**, will fill you completely with joy and peace because you trust in him. Then you will overflow with confident **hope** through the power of the Holy Spirit" (Romans 15:13 NLT, author's emphasis).

Looking back, I see how God had His hand on me. It still brings joy to my heart, tears to my eyes, and a lump in my throat. Where would I be if my heavenly Father had not encouraged me to turn my attention back on the One who is able and promises to work all things for my good? He will always be and always has been my only hope. Mercy rewrote my life, and I won't ever forget it!

PRAISE BREAK

Right now. Right here. I have to take another praise break and thank the Lord for His kindness and faithfulness to me. I couldn't earn it, and I sure don't deserve it, but He has shown up over and over again in my life. I cannot thank Him enough. And the fact that you are reading this book is proof that He keeps showing up in your life. Take the time to thank Him for His faithfulness to you.

SIGNPOST

Let's stop and take a minute to look and see if we can find a signpost on this **path** we're on. Which letter in the acronym do you think best fits the influence and power of speaking God's Word over your life? It takes humility and surrendering to believe God's truth rather than our feelings. But that is where the power of walking by faith will always be found. We can do and say what's right even when life is all wrong. So, I am going to choose the letter H. When we *humble* ourselves, turn from evil, and live a life of *holiness* for the Lord, He always pours out His grace, and we will go down a **PATH** that will lead to inner **HEALING**.

Chapter 5

SILENCE THE SERPENT

Life will have hard days. Jesus said that on this side of heaven, we will have trials, but every valley we walk through has a promise from Him. Every shadow has an end, and dark days will not last forever. I have a dear friend who is a pastor's wife in northern Iowa. In 2008, her husband became deathly ill and needed a kidney transplant to survive. Her church was praying. Our church was praying. Saints around the globe were praying for him to be healed, but he got sicker and sicker. A bitter weed sprang up in her soul. In her most vulnerable moment, the accuser of the brethren attacked her mind. While Satan has and will always be less powerful than our God, he continues to steal, kill, and destroy, "for the accuser of our brethren, who accused them before our God day and night, has been cast down" (Revelation 12:10 NKJV).

She said she could almost hear the hiss of the serpent as he whispered in her ear, "Does Jesus care?"

And in the middle of the enemy's attack, she cried, "Jesus!"

Immediately the Holy Spirit replied, "Jesus does care!"

Satan refused to give up and said, "Does God hear you?"

The Spirit responded again, "God does hear you."

She said the enemy and the Holy Spirit were using the very same words, but they were arranged in a different order. Isn't that just like the enemy? He twists the truths from God's Word and tries to discourage and defeat God's people.

That pastor's wife rose to her feet and shouted, "It's time to silence the serpent!"

The Lord spoke to her again, "I am taking you and your husband on a missionary journey that you will never forget. Your husband is going to go through the surgery, and it will be successful. Every prayer that people prayed for healing will go toward his recovery."

How did she know God heard her? She had hidden the Scriptures in her heart and trusted the voice of truth over the clamoring voice of depression. Just as David said so long ago, "The righteous cry out, and the LORD hears them; / he delivers them from all their troubles" (Psalm 34:17 NIV).

God kept His Word. He heard this ministry couple's cry. This pastor's life and ministry wasn't over. He is still pastoring and declaring God's truths seventeen years later. Glory to God!

DECLARE TRUTH

For you to be able to silence the serpent, you must know the Word of God. This is so important. You must be spiritually equipped to face the enemy. You are in a war. You will need the full armor of God. Paul goes into detail to describe this armor, but meditate on just one verse for now. "Take the helmet of salvation and the sword of the Spirit, which is the word of God" (Ephesians 6:17 NIV). This Scripture calls God's Word the "sword of the Spirit." When we know and declare Scripture, it has the power to cut through the enemy's lies and render the enemy powerless. Keep declaring truth over your life.

THE JOY OF THE LORD IS YOUR STRENGTH

Depression is at an all-time high in our society. Satan uses discouragement, hopelessness, and despair to try to defeat God's people. How we need spiritual weapons of warfare to fight these battles! One of the greatest weapons we can possess is the joy of the Lord. Why do we need joy? Because the joy of the Lord is our strength—see how it is described in Nehemiah! "And Nehemiah continued, 'Go and celebrate with a feast of rich foods and sweet drinks, and share gifts of food with people who have nothing prepared. This is a sacred day before our Lord. Don't be dejected and sad, for the joy of the LORD is your strength!'" (Nehemiah 8:10 NLT).

Spiritual joy is deep cheerfulness and gladness of heart. Joy is having our spirit in a state of calm. This joy comes from a direct result of knowing Jesus personally and accepting the finished work that He's done and will do for us, not just in this life but in the life to come. So, joy isn't forced upon us; we have to make a deliberate decision in the middle of life's most difficult circumstances to trust the One who gives us His joy deep down in our souls.

When our hope is in God, joy always follows. Think about it. One of the benefits of wholly following the Lord is that joys are traveling day and night just to get to us. When I understood this and where my joy came from, it was a game changer. Right in the middle of uncertainty, dysfunctional relationships, and overwhelming grief, I could still choose joy.

When I physically couldn't see any clear **path** to victory . . .

When the medical doctor's words were, "I hate to tell you this unfortunate news, but . . . "

When I received the devastating news that our daughter was deceased (although I had spoken with her earlier in the day) . . .

God was still with me and would walk with me through every deep, dark, and low valley. Just knowing He is with us through every tsunami should cause our hearts to rejoice. This knowledge changes how we look at every trial. We don't have to go through any heartache alone.

Listen to me. In the middle of midnight tears, I sought the Lord, and He heard and answered me. It was right there that I found joy that gave me strength to overcome.

You aren't called to be overcome by trauma, abuse, neglect, or anything else that's been in your past. You are called to overcome it. God has called you to be an overcomer. He will use your story to bring healing to others. You will live and see God turn your tears into showers of blessing. He will redeem every teardrop because He is the Redeemer of the rain! Hear the sweet verse of this song as it says, "Weeping may endure for a night, but joy cometh in the morning" (Psalm 30:5 KJV).

CHOOSE JOY

I knew I was on a **path** to victory when I discovered this biblical truth. Our troubles, concerns, mess-ups, relationship failures, outward status in the eyes of the world, unexpected death announcements, and physical and mental health challenges do not dictate our joy. Remember this truth—the joy of the Lord is not dependent upon our outward circumstances. It is a heart issue. Let's choose joy in every season of life we're in right now.

This sound biblical teaching helped me so much. I made a decision to align my trajectory with the apostle James: "Consider it nothing but joy, my brothers and sisters, whenever you fall into various trials. Be assured that the testing of your faith [through experience] produces endurance [leading to spiritual maturity, and inner peace]. And let endurance have its perfect result and do a thorough work, so that you may be perfect and completely developed [in your faith], lacking in nothing" (James 1:2–4 AMP).

PRAISE BREAK

Oh, this blesses my soul. When I think of where Jesus brought me from, gratitude rises up inside me. I have to take another praise break and thank the Lord for the joy He has blessed me with. If I allowed my childhood trauma to reign in my mind and heart, I could be on the floor in a fetal position sucking my thumb, but Jesus calls me higher. Because of Him, I can stand upright. I can face today and tomorrow with my head held high and never be ashamed of the One who is the Difference Maker. I refuse to give the enemy any free rent in my head. Jesus has caused me to triumph over the past. I owe Him all the praise and honor I can bestow upon Him.

He wants you to stand tall and praise Him for all the ways He is working in your life right now. He is worthy of all praise. As Paul wrote to the people of Corinth, "Now thanks be to God who always leads us in triumph in Christ, and through us diffuses the fragrance of His knowledge in every place" (2 Corinthians 2:14 NKJV).

PRAYER JOURNAL

You've reached another prayer journal spot, a time to slow down and soak in God's Word. Remember, in order to silence the serpent, you must be prepared with God's truths. It's time to declare truth again over your life with these life-giving Scriptures. Just as you did last time, be sure to insert your name. It will increase your faith for your family and your situation.

> For thou wilt not leave <u>my</u> soul to Sheol;
> Neither wilt thou suffer thy holy one to see corruption.
> Thou wilt show <u>me</u> the **path** of life:
> In thy presence is fulness of joy;
> In thy right hand there are pleasures for evermore.
> (Psalm 16:10–11 ASV, author's emphasis)

Look at this same verse in the Amplified Translation: "You will show <u>me</u> the **path** of life; / In Your presence is fullness of joy; / In Your right hand there are pleasures forevermore" (Psalm 16:11 AMP, author's emphasis).

"Hear, O LORD, when I cry aloud; / Be gracious and compassionate to me and answer me" (Psalm 27:7 AMP, author's emphasis).

"<u>My</u> lips shall shout for joy when I sing praises to You, and <u>my</u> inner being, which You have redeemed" (Psalm 71:23 AMPC, author's emphasis).

"Casting the whole of <u>your</u> care [all <u>your</u> anxieties, all <u>your</u> worries, all <u>your</u> concerns, once and for all] on Him, for He cares for <u>you</u> affectionately and cares about <u>you</u> watchfully" (1 Peter 5:7 AMPC, author's emphasis).

Even when it doesn't look like God's working, He is. We need His grace to help us stay on the potter's wheel for the refiner to complete the work in us. Weeping may endure for the night, but a harvest of joy comes in the morning, because His mercies are new every morning (Lamentations 3:22–23, author's paraphrase). Good mornings come with the mercy of our Lord!

SIGNPOST

Let's stop and take a minute to look and see if we can find a signpost on the **path** we find ourselves on in this chapter. Which letter in the acronym do you think best fits the ability to silence the serpent that comes from the influence of abiding in the Vine and bearing spiritual fruit for the Lord? The joy of the Lord keeps us grounded through all the storms of life that may be thrown at us by Satan and the sin that is part of this world. This fruit of the Spirit is a vital anchor in our spiritual life. So, I am going to choose the letter A. When we live close to Jesus and seek His presence throughout the day, we will discover it to be an *anchored ambassador* that will lead us down a **PATH** that leads us to spiritual **ALIGNMENT**.

Chapter 6

TRUST AND OBEY

And a great road will go through that once deserted land.
It will be named the Highway of Holiness.
Evil-minded people will never travel on it.
It will be only for those who walk in God's ways;
fools will never walk there.
(Isaiah 35:8 NLT)

What does it mean to **obey**? I'm glad you asked. To **obey** means to comply with the command, direction, or request of someone and submit to their authority. I know that as I deal with mortal man, just the word *obey* can bring some uneasiness to my heart. When you've gone through emotional, mental, and physical abuse, just hearing this word causes internal rebellion to arise! But I have great news for you. Our God isn't like a mortal man. So, it becomes comforting to know the One who says, "'For I know the plans I have for you,' says the LORD. 'They are plans for good and not for disaster, to give you a future and a hope'" (Jeremiah 29:11 NLT). So, this is our good, good Father, and He only wants to do good by us.

You need to remember that this promise is only available to those who **trust** and **obey** Him according to His Word.

This verse from Isaiah speaks of a road that is kept for God's people who **trust** and **obey** His Word. But what must you do before you **obey** someone?

Healthy relationships must have a foundation of **trust** before each party agrees (consciously or not) to **obey** the other. This type of **trust** means to believe in the reliability, truth, ability, and strength of something or someone. **Trust** for the born-again believer is felt most deeply in God and in His Word. However, this type of believing doesn't give us an automatic exempt card from anxiety, mess-ups, dysfunctional family relationships, unexpected death announcements, medical tests, and other difficult challenges. Individually, we have to **trust** and **obey** God's Word no matter how long it takes. His Word has the power to settle us no matter what is happening around us because His Word will never change. "Forever, O LORD, Your word is settled in heaven [standing firm and unchangeable]" (Psalm 119:89 AMP).

When we build our lives on the forever unshakeable foundation, we will have the needed courage, fortitude, and confidence to **trust** that God won't fail us. The Bible says that God cannot lie. This is a biblical truth we can **trust**. We can **trust** God's character to be sovereign and constant "by two unchangeable things [His promise and His oath] in which it is impossible for God to lie, we who have fled [to Him] for refuge would have strong encouragement and indwelling strength to hold tightly to the hope set before us" (Hebrews 6:18 AMP).

You might *still* be asking, "What can we **trust**?" We can **trust** God to always keep His Word. Through your faith and knowledge of the Scriptures, **trust** that He loves you and has a good plan with His expected end for you!

THE PHONE CALL

We received a call that no parent ever wants to hear. Unfortunately, I wasn't available to answer, so a voice message asked us to return the call. Before this could be completed, we received another call with the heart-wrenching news: "Your daughter is dead!"

Words are inadequate. They cannot ever describe how low our spirits sank or how our hearts ached. We hoped to hear they had made a mistake, and we could wake up from this horrific nightmare, but it wasn't a false alarm. Our daughter was gone. We cried until we had no more tears. Life had changed in a split second, and our lives would never be the same.

So, where do we go when life doesn't make sense? Why do bad things happen to good people? How do we prepare our hearts when our world has been riveted by such sad news and our hope has been shaken? How do we **trust** a God who said He would never leave us or abandon us? I'll tell you what I did.

I made a determined effort that fear would not dominate my thoughts. I knew the **path** I was called to be on even in the trenches of grief. I had to guard my mind against any unbelieving thoughts. I had to doubt my doubts and believe that God is trustworthy, righteous, reliable, just, and faithful. In order to fully **trust** and **obey** God, I had to lean into Scripture. In Paul's and Timothy's letter to the Philippians, they wrote this encouragement: "Finally, brethren, whatsoever things are true, whatsoever things are honest, whatsoever things are just, whatsoever things are pure, whatsoever things are lovely, whatsoever things are of good report; if there be any virtue, and if there be any praise, think on these things" (Philippians 4:8 KJV).

I made a deliberate decision to **trust** the Lord even when I didn't understand. I had to say with dear Brother Job, "Though He slay me, yet will I **trust** Him" (Job 13:15 NKJV, author's emphasis). That deliberate decision was only possible because I had walked with the Lord long enough to know that there were promises in His Word for every season of life. He had provided weapons for spiritual warfare, and I needed every one of them. So, I started by putting on the full armor of God—I realized I needed a shield of faith to extinguish all the flaming arrows the enemy shot at me (Ephesians 6:16, author's paraphrase). In the book of Ephesians, Paul goes into great detail for the armor of God. This may not be one of our Prayer Journal sections, but I want you to look up Ephesians 6! You may need to highlight the armor that is going to guide you on the **path** toward **trust** and obedience in the midst of whatever trials you are facing. In the days following that horrible phone call, I had to "put on the full armor of God, so that [I could] take [my] stand against the devil's schemes" (Ephesians 6:11 NIV).

I got out my Bible, pen, and journal and went to warring in the spirit realm. I knew before I even started that victory belongs to Jesus, and that same victory belongs to me. I had read the back of God's Book, and we win!

The Bible is the most wonderfully profound Book. There are Scriptures to comfort us when we lose a loved one. The book of 2 Samuel documents the loss of David and Bathsheba's infant in chapter twelve: "David prayed to God for the baby. David fasted and went into his house and stayed there, lying on the ground all night. The elders of David's family came to him and tried to pull him up from the ground, but he refused to get up or to eat food with them" (2 Samuel 12:16–17 NCV). When we read these verses, we see David's despair. God has given us these accounts so that we can see His character and how He leads His children out of pain. After David's son had died, he cleaned himself up and went to worship God. At that point, "David said, 'While the baby was still alive, I fasted, and I cried. I thought, "Who knows? Maybe the Lord will feel sorry for me and let the baby live." But now that the baby is dead, why should I fast? I can't bring him back to life. Someday I will go to him, but he cannot come back to me'" (2 Samuel 12:22–23 NCV).

Our daughter was gone. My husband and I couldn't bring her back, but one day we would go to be with her. Our thoughts had truly become a mirror to David's response in verse 23. We knew we had to anchor our faith on the truths of God's Word. So, that's what we did. We discovered and experienced the power in every promise.

PRAISE BREAK

When I think back on that dark night of my soul and how faithful Jesus was to me, I have to stop and raise my hands and voice and take a praise break. Won't you join me? The Lord has been so faithful to you too. Thank Him for the storms He has brought you through. He is worthy of our praise!

PRAYER JOURNAL

You've reached another opportunity to slow down, take out a journal, pen, or highlighter, and soak up verses from the Bible that will call you into this opportunity to **trust** and **obey** God! I encourage you to continue inserting your name in each promise to make it more real to your heart.

"It is better to take refuge in the LORD / Than to **trust** in man" (Psalm 118:8 AMP, author's emphasis).

"If <u>ye</u> be willing and obedient, <u>ye</u> shall eat the good of the land" (Isaiah 1:19 KJV, author's emphasis).

"For I know the thoughts that I think toward <u>you</u>, saith the LORD, thoughts of peace, and not of evil, to give <u>you</u> an expected end" (Jeremiah 29:11 KJV, author's emphasis).

"I am the Lord <u>your</u> God, who brought <u>you</u> out of the land of Egypt to give <u>you</u> the land of Canaan and to be <u>your</u> God" (Leviticus 25:38 NLT, author's emphasis).

"As soon as Jesus heard the word that was spoken, he saith unto the ruler of the synagogue, Be not afraid, only believe" (Mark 5:36 KJV).

BACK TO THE PHONE CALL

When I began standing on the truth of God's Word, I immediately recognized that the same God who brought me to it would also bring me through it. I learned that God didn't just call me to **trust** and **obey** Him in the good times, but in the hard times too. Even when the fire was turned up seven times hotter and the flames were lapping around me, my God carried me through every situation. Yes, I grieved our daughter's passing, but I was able to be functional. God granted me extra grace. There was no smell of smoke on me. God didn't put out the fire, but He placed Jesus in the fire with me. You will see this imagery of smoke and fire again in the next chapter, and I want you to think about the command to **trust** and **obey** God then as well.

I must repeat this truth to you. I believe you are not reading my book by chance. God has placed it in your hands. So, listen to me. The season you are walking through right now, remember this: It's not about God putting out all your fires; it's about Him being in the fire with you. And that will make all the difference in your walk of faith.

HISTORY LESSON

When you belong to Jesus, it doesn't matter what news may come your way. You must let your trusting heart sing of God's faithfulness. Even if the news is devastating, He is with you. He is trustworthy, and He will lead you to a **path** of victory. Nothing can separate you from the love of God. Every valley has a promise. You can walk in complete victory even in the valley because He is with you.

Even though I walk
through the darkest valley,
I will fear no evil,
for you are with me;
your rod and your staff,
they comfort me.
(Psalm 23:4 NIV)

MY RESCUER

There are other times in my life that God has worked supernatural miracles. He rescued me from complete devastation. Earlier I spoke briefly about how God supernaturally healed me in South Africa and even the medical doctors had to testify. No God like my God! This was one of the many times He saved my life when medically all external scans or tests showed I could have been dead. BUT He continued to bring me through every health concern and has given me wholeness, wellness, and soundness through every storm. That is why I testify my God is still speaking to the wind and the waves and saying, "Peace, be still" (Mark 4:39 KJV). I recall that when there wasn't anything in the cupboard or the refrigerator to eat, my God sent manna from heaven, just as He did for the children of Israel. My siblings and I may not have been eating manna from heaven—just look up Exodus 16:35— but we were provided for by our heavenly Father. So, for this and so much more, I will never give up on God or accuse Him of being unfaithful because of a trial I might have faced. Why? Because I have tried Him for myself, and I know whatever it takes to bring my feet on a **path** to safe landing, He will do it! There are things that are impossible to man, but with my God all things are possible (Matthew 19:26, author's paraphrase)! He never has failed me and never will fail me. He is and will always be my Great Physician and Rescuer. The Lord has set up His kingdom in our hearts to let us know that He is our hope that brings joy, and as we **trust** Him, we will begin living in peace.

PRAYER JOURNAL

You might be thinking, "I already had a prayer journal break for chapter six." Well, you're right . . . you did! But this chapter needs a second one! I want you to really meditate on the truth that God is your Rescuer. Take that journal and pen or highlighter back out! Speak this next verse over your life and circumstances!

"Then we cried out, 'Lord, help <u>us</u>! Rescue <u>us</u>!' And he did! God spoke the words 'Be healed,' and <u>we</u> were healed, delivered from death's door!" (Psalm 107:19–20 TPT, author's emphasis).

SIGNPOST

What signpost do you see on this **path** of **trust**? Which letter in the acronym do you think best fits the choice to seek the Lord and **obey** His Word in the midst of trials and pain? When we stand on the *timeless truths* of the Lord and **trust** His Word, we will find our foundation is secure to build our lives on. So, no matter how hard the storms may blow, we will still be standing after the storm. Trust is a fundamental weapon in our spiritual life. So, I am going to choose the letter T. When we **trust** in the Lord with all our heart, that will lead us down a **PATH** that leads us to complete **TRANSFORMATION**. We will never be the same. We are being made into the image of Christ each day. Just as Paul and Timothy wrote to the people of Corinth, "And we all, with unveiled face, continually seeing as in a mirror the glory of the Lord, are progressively being transformed into His image from [one degree of] glory to [even more] glory, which comes from the Lord, [who is] the Spirit" (2 Corinthians 3:18 AMP).

Chapter 7

PEACE

The Hebrew word *shalom* means "God Himself is our **peace**." God's gift to every born-again believer is spiritual health. Nothing is broken. We can walk in spiritual wholeness. His blood breaks the curse of sin that caused disease in our soul. There is a clarity from right and wrong thinking. There is no confusion. What God calls sin, we call sin. What God calls holiness, we call holiness. This spiritual soundness only comes from being in right standing with God and each other. When the Prince of **Peace** rules in our hearts and minds, we will be blessed by a **peace** that passes all understanding. Toward the end of Jesus's earthly ministry, He tried to comfort His disciples. He said to them, "**Peace** I leave with you; My [own] **peace** I now give and bequeath to you. Not as the world gives do I give to you. Do not let your hearts be troubled, neither let them be afraid. [Stop allowing yourselves to be agitated and disturbed; and do not permit yourselves to be fearful and intimidated and cowardly and unsettled]" (John 14:27 AMPC, author's emphasis). Years later, Paul also wrote of **peace** in his letter to the Philippians. He closed out this letter with words that have now become a commonly quoted Scripture on **peace**: "And the **peace** of God, which passeth all understanding, shall keep your hearts and minds through Christ Jesus" (Philippians 4:7 KJV).

Peace can be present in the midst of calm circumstances, but it can also be present in the midst of chaos and turmoil. Sound the battle cry. Now it's time to declare war on the enemy. Rise up and let the enemy know that God has made you brave. Send out this resounding message to the dark forces of evil that have been sent to bind you—"Back off, devil. It won't work this time because I know the Wheel in the middle of the wheel. The Prince of **Peace** lives inside me. I rest in this truth and His **peace**."

The world, people, and circumstances can never give us **peace**, and they cannot take it away.

Even when you don't see it, God is at work behind the scenes on your behalf. Oh, it's true. He has a plan for your life. Maybe the accuser of the brethren is condemning you right now. He likes to point out our weaknesses and failures, but lean in close and listen. Failure isn't final with the Father. Your story will not end in ashes. Just commit all your sins and mistakes under the blood. Then, stand still and watch God move. Just as Paul wrote to his mentee Timothy, "If we are unfaithful, / he remains faithful, / for he cannot deny who he is" (2 Timothy 2:13 NLT).

THE PRICE OF PEACE

While rereading through my journals, I begin to see a pattern. I have often wondered why things that are sent to try to disturb my **peace** always seem to come early in the morning. While thinking about so many of my life stories, I recall many of these before-daybreak trials. The old saints called it the midnight hour or the dark night of the soul. Have you cried midnight tears? Have you ever felt your **peace** disturbed? I know I have, but I have learned that if it costs me my **peace**, it is too expensive. Never let anyone or anything steal your **peace**. Trust that God is sovereign and everything that comes your way has been measured by the Father's hand of grace.

I remember early one morning noticing a call waiting on my phone. Several days earlier, I had gone through several physical health challenges. So, I immediately thought this phone message might be from my medical doctor. Words don't adequately describe the fear, anxiety, and all of the "what ifs" that tormented my heart and mind. Although I hadn't even listened to the voice message, the flashing light was speaking volumes. At this time, we had a decorative cuckoo clock that automatically made musical sounds when chiming the time between 7:00 a.m. and 7:00 p.m.

Yes, you guessed it. That cuckoo clock sounded and announced the hour of the day was 2:00 a.m. Immediately, my heart started pounding. A cold sweat formed on my forehead. The fear factor was real in that room, but I also understood that the Prince of **Peace** lives inside me. **Peace** of mind was at my disposal. So, it took every ounce of courage I could find to turn from Satan's tormenting lies. I reached out in faith, touched the Lord, and shouted, "I won't let You go until I see a healing deliverance concerning this matter." Fast forward after one round of radiation, and God supernaturally healed me!

PRAISE BREAK

I can't stop praising Him for all the kindness and goodness He has bestowed on my life! I have to take another praise break and thank the Lord. He has blessed me again and again. Thank You, Jesus! Take this moment to offer a sacrifice of praise for the ways God has showered you with His kindness and led you into a **peace** that only He can provide.

PRAYER JOURNAL

Dear friend, you have reached another opportunity to write in your prayer journal or even make notes in this book's pages! Slow down and read over these verses. Use God's own words to speak **peace** over yourself in this moment!

> God, you're such a safe and powerful place to find refuge! You're a proven help in time of trouble—more than enough and always available whenever I need you. So we will never fear even if every structure of support were to crumble away. We will not fear even when the earthquakes and shakes, moving mountains and casting them into the sea. For the raging roar of stormy winds and crashing waves cannot erode our faith in you. *Pause in his presence.* (Psalm 46:1–3 TPT, author's emphasis)

> He who dwells in the shelter of the Most High
> Will remain secure and rest in the shadow of

the Almighty [whose power no enemy can withstand].

I will say of the Lord, "He is my refuge and my fortress, My God, in whom I trust [with great confidence, and on whom I rely]!" (Psalm 91:1–2 AMP)

Do not be anxious or worried about anything, but in everything [every circumstance and situation] by prayer and petition with thanksgiving, continue to make your [specific] requests known to God. And the **peace** of God [that **peace** which reassures the heart, that **peace**] which transcends all understanding, [that **peace** which] stands guard over your hearts and your minds in Christ Jesus [is yours]. (Philippians 4:6 7 NLT, author's emphasis)

STUFF OF LIFE

I want to be very real and authentic in the pages of this book. I'm not desiring to paint a picture that since I have given my life to Jesus, I don't have any problems. I still walk through the hard stuff of life just like you do. I face physical issues, family problems, dysfunctional relationships, deep grief, and other challenges that are part of the human experience in this broken world, but the Prince of **Peace** lives inside me. He feels what I feel. He is acquainted with all my ways. He understands that I am made of dust (Psalm 103:14, author's paraphrase), but His grace is sufficient for me and His power will work through my weakness. Paul explained this to the people of Corinth too. Paul begged God to take away his pain, and "each time he said, 'My grace is all you need. My power works best in weakness.' So now I am glad to boast about my weaknesses, so that the power of Christ can work through me" (2 Corinthians 12:9 NLT). I know He will use His power through your weakness too. We have His Word on it!

Feeling a real, deep **peace** may seem just out of reach on many days. We have God's Word and the promises that can be found there, but we also have our knowledge of the Son of God. While He understands us, we have the privilege of learning to understand Him as well! The book of Hebrews puts it so well: "So then, since we have a great High Priest who has entered heaven, Jesus the Son of God, let us hold firmly to what we believe. This High Priest of ours understands our weaknesses, for he faced all of the same testings we do, yet he did not sin. So let us come boldly to the throne of our gracious God. There we will receive his mercy, and we will find grace to help us when we need it most" (Hebrews 4:14–16 NLT).

EVEN IF

Back in chapter six I told you that God granted me extra grace when I received a phone call that brought pain and desolation. He didn't put out the fire, but He did place Jesus in the fire with me, and as I said, there was no smell of smoke on me. That painful time in my life gave me a new appreciation for what happened to Daniel's friends. I testify to the same proclamation that the three Hebrew boys did when they were thrown in the fiery furnace. These young men from Judah had such amazing faith that their

peace was not even shaken when they were threatened with being burned alive! My God, and your God, is the same holy Redeemer of Shadrach, Meshach, and Abednego. My God is able to deliver me from any physical problem, emotional issue, or whatever trouble I might face, *but even if He does not*, I will not bow down or turn my back on my God!

"Shadrach, Meshach, and Abed-nego answered the king, 'O Nebuchadnezzar, we do not need to answer you on this point. If it be so, our God whom we serve is able to rescue us from the furnace of blazing fire, and He will rescue us from your hand, O king. But even if He does not, let it be known to you, O king, that we are not going to serve your gods or worship the golden image that you have set up!'" (Daniel 3:16–18 AMP).

How blessed we are! God has given us the precious and coveted gift of **peace**. Even when we don't see a way of escape, God is at work. Sometimes He calms the storm, and sometimes He calms us. He keeps us in a resting **peace** when we keep our minds stayed on Him. May we never allow fear, intimidation, or anxiety to take root in our lives. We belong to the Lord. May His Holy Spirit reign with great **peace** in our lives. Just as Isaiah's prophetic words say, "You will guard him and keep him in perfect and constant **peace** whose mind [both its inclination and its character] is stayed on You, because he commits himself to You, leans on You, and hopes confidently in You" (Isaiah 26:3 AMPC, author's emphasis). The Word of God spoken through Isaiah points to Jesus again and again. In Jesus's mighty name, amen!

SIGNPOST

What signpost do you see on this **path** of **peace**? Which letter in the acronym do you think best leads to walking in **peace** through every season of life? You may think, "Well, I can see a few letters from **PATH** that make sense here!" The Bible makes it clear that God will keep us in perfect **peace** when we keep our mind on Him. So, I am going to choose the letter P. When we *pray* and *persevere* to keep our hearts and minds fixed on the Lord, that will lead us down a **PATH** that leads us to the divine **PURPOSE** and destiny that God has for us.

Again, I want to share a verse from the apostle Paul. He wrote to the Romans of this perseverance—he urged them to seek the Spirit over their flesh. "The mind governed by the flesh is death, but the mind governed by the Spirit is life and **peace**" (Romans 8:6 NIV, author's emphasis).

Chapter 8

OLD PATHS AND NEW PATHS

This is what the LORD says:

"Stand at the crossroads and look;
ask for the *ancient* **paths**,
ask where the good way is, and walk in it,
and you will find rest for your souls.
But you said, 'We will not walk in it.'"
(Jeremiah 6:16 NIV, author's emphasis)

In this Scripture we are encouraged to ask for the *ancient* **paths**. Why do you think that is? We need the *old* **paths** because they contain *timeless truths*. Asking for these *ancient* or *old* **paths** isn't enough, though; we are also told to walk in them because that is where the good way is. It's where we will find rest for our souls too. What a promise in God's Word!

I realize this Scripture is a command from the Lord to the people of Israel. They were at a crossroads and had to make a choice of whether they would follow the Lord or go their own way. How it must grieve God's heart when we insist on having our own way instead of following the **path** He has for us. You might be asking, "How will I know I am following the Lord and on the right **path**?" Well, the first thing we must do is acknowledge Him. That's what His Word teaches. Solomon is believed to be the author of the book of Proverbs, and it makes sense that a man who asked God for wisdom would have thought, "In all thy ways acknowledge him, and he shall direct thy **paths**" (Proverbs 3:6 KJV, author's emphasis).

If we want the Lord to direct our **paths**, He must have preeminence in our lives. We must honor Him and make room for Him. "And He is the head of the body, the church: who is the beginning, the firstborn from the dead; that in all things He may have the preeminence" (Colossians 1:18 KJV). Do you need the same reminder that the Colossians had to hear?

There are unchanging biblical truths that will never change, even in this ever-changing world. So, beware of smooth talkers. The *ancient* **paths** will keep us grounded in a world full of sinking sand. We will never outgrow our need for the Lord. The Good News of Jesus Christ never loses its luster. There are landmarks and signposts on these *ancient* **paths**. One of the landmarks is the cross of Calvary. It will always declare that we are lost and in need of a Savior. We will always need His sinless blood to wash our sins away.

Never stray from these fundamental truths found on the *ancient* **paths**. People may call you old-fashioned and out of touch with the times. That's okay. You are in touch with the King of kings. Some of the views on the *ancient* **path** may not be popular. That's okay too. You keep standing for truth and following the Lord. This **path** will lead you to a wonderful destination. Jesus spoke of the **path** to heaven—He spoke this truth bluntly. "You can enter God's Kingdom only through the narrow gate. The highway to hell is broad, and its gate is wide for the many who choose that way" (Matthew 7:13 NLT).

Sin always takes us farther than we intended to go. It makes us pay far more than we intended too. It keeps us bound longer than we ever imagined. Oh, there is safety on the *ancient* **paths**.

Looking over my life, I can see how my grandmothers' faith and prayers carried me. They intentionally followed the narrow, *ancient* way. Their choice affects my life still today. While I honor my grandmothers' faith and respect their walk with the Lord, I still had to choose Jesus for myself. I couldn't be *grandmothered* into the kingdom. I had to have my own personal encounter with the Lord.

TRAILBLAZER FOR JESUS ONTO A NEW PATH

So, while I am traveling down the *ancient* **path**, I discover that I am blazing a *new* **path** too. We are all called to be trailblazers for Jesus. We have the power, in Christ, to blaze a trail for others to follow. The future for your family, no matter what your background is, can be influenced by the **path** you blaze.

There is something very precious and comforting when we walk in the *old* **paths**, but there is also a holy excitement when we discover the *new* **paths** God has carved out for each of His children through the *timeless truths* of His Word.

We might call these **paths** fresh beginnings, another chance, divine purpose, or God's purpose for us. *New* **paths** don't usually feel familiar, but God uses them to deepen our faith and draw us closer to Him.

PATHS OF JUSTICE

For those of us who have endured abuse or neglect in our childhood, God often has us walk down **paths** of justice. Many ask why they must wait for that justice, but we may never understand the Lord's timing or full plan. "Therefore the Lord will wait, that He may be gracious to you; / And therefore He will be exalted, that He may have mercy on you. / For the Lord is a God of justice; / Blessed are all those who wait for Him" (Isaiah 30:18 NKJV). Do you see that last part? God will bless you when you wait for Him and His timed justice. You won't have to lift a finger to redeem your story, but the mighty Redeemer will be working behind the scenes to bring total redemption. Those who walk this **path** usually find themselves standing up for the oppressed. They are a voice for the voiceless, fulfilling a biblical command.

God has used His people to speak His truths for thousands of years. He used Micah to say,

> He has shown you, O man, what is good;
> And what does the Lord require of you
> But to do justly,
> To love mercy,
> And to walk humbly with your God?
> (Micah 6:8 NKJV)

When we walk humbly with our God down the **path** of justice, we will find it is marked by His presence. He is near to the brokenhearted. He leads us by His hand. It might not look like it at first, but this **path** is a **path** of forgiveness. Don't misunderstand. This doesn't mean the people who have abused us will get away with what they've done and be a major part of our lives. We need healthy boundaries. And God has a big spank paddle. He is a righteous Judge. But we can never walk in the freedom we are called to walk in unless we forgive and leave all bitterness behind. There is a freedom in forgiveness that brings mental, spiritual, and physical health. Paul set a high standard for the Romans who received his letter. It may seem like a nearly impossible standard, but it also shows us how high God is on that rung of power. "Do not repay anyone evil for evil. Be careful to do what is right in the eyes of everyone. If it is possible, as far as it depends on you, live at peace with everyone. Do not take revenge, my dear friends, but leave room for God's wrath, for it is written: 'It is mine to avenge; I will repay,' says the Lord" (Romans 12:17–19 NIV).

THE HIGHWAY OF HOLINESS

This chapter has touched on *ancient* **paths**, *old* and *new* **paths**, trailblazers, and **paths** of justice. Now let's look at something even higher! If you open up your Bible to Isaiah 35, you may see a heading like "Joy of the Redeemed" or "Hope for Restoration"! God used Isaiah to show the promise that was there for His true people.

> And a great road will go through that once deserted land.
> It will be named the Highway of Holiness.

Evil-minded people will never travel on it.
It will be only for those who walk in God's ways;
fools will never walk there.
(Isaiah 35:8 NLT)

God may have used Isaiah to initially share these words with the Israelites, but His Word is speaking it to you today. One of the *new* **paths** for some first-generational believers is a **path** of holiness. This is a road that leads to complete transformation. Our wise heavenly Father purifies our motives and hearts. He even renews our minds. Everything that we need, He will always be.

WALKING FORWARD

My prayer for you, dear reader, is that you see the importance of combining the *ancient* **paths** with the *new*. They will anchor you in the *timeless truths* that we so desperately need. You will be personally challenged by the lessons on each **path**. The victories you gain will help you soar into the next season of your life. God designs each **path** to lead you closer to Him.

You and I are not just travelers on these **paths**; we are guides for those who come after us. As we walk faithfully, we leave behind footprints of faith for the next generation. Let us walk boldly on the *old* and *new* **paths** God has set before us, trusting that His way is always good and His destination is always glorious.

A PRAYER FOR THE CHILDREN ON GOD'S PATH

It has been an honor to speak into your life. Before I close the pages in this book, I want to encourage you to trust the process and the **path** God has you on at this time. If we don't complete the process His way, we will find ourselves blaming God and becoming trapped in a revolving door. I say, "Rise up, holy men and women of God!" Allow God to finish what He's started. We must know all our life is measured through His hands! Just as Moses said, I also say unto you:

> "Today God has given you the choice between life and death, between blessings and curses. Now I call on heaven and earth to witness the choice you make. Oh, that you would choose life, so that you and your descendants might live! You can make this choice by loving the LORD your God, obeying him, and committing yourself firmly to him. This is the key to living in God's abundant life in every area. And if you love and obey the Lord, you will live long in the land that the Lord swore to give your ancestors Abraham, Isaac, and Jacob." (Deuteronomy 30:19–20 NLT)

Travel light and enjoy the journey on your **path** to freedom.

PRAYER

Friends, I am a woman of prayer! I know that I just shared one of Moses's prayers for the Israelites, but I want to share this one from my own heart with you!

Heavenly Father, thank You for giving us Your Son, the Prince of Peace. Lord Jesus, thank You for being our peace even when we don't see a way of escape. Please help us to believe that You are our Rescuer! You promise to keep our minds in a resting peace as we keep our minds stayed on You. Now, give us Your strength and courage to embrace every corridor of change when it's presented. Give us a greater capacity for Your presence. Let Your Spirit flow through us in every season of our lives. We trust Your sovereign hand to lead us down **paths** of righteousness for Your name's sake. We ask that fear, insecurity, intimidation, and anxiety would not control our thoughts or lives. We pray we will never be overcome with evil, but overcome evil with good. We thank You for the work of the Holy Spirit being freely released in our lives and making us more like You. Just as it says in the Gospel of John, help us to decrease so You may increase more and more in our lives. Make us overcomers for Your honor and glory. Amen.

CONCLUSION

I am living, moving, breathing, and devouring the Word of God daily. I look forward to the day when I will see my mother Catherine, my father Timothy, my dad Spurgeon, my grandmothers Annie Mae and Annie Laura, my daddy Mr. Boykin, my daddy Mr. Williams, my daddy Mr. Walter Jr., my uncle/daddy Tommie, my mother Mrs. Eunice, my mother Willie Earl, my best friend Sister Brozine, my other best friend Rosetta, our daughter Punkin'-Amoyiah (The Doctor), and our great-grandson Justin (Red). I am confident each of you are walking in divine health on streets paved with real gold.

I am so very thankful to God for each one of you. I am grateful for the love, care, and influence you were and still are in my life. Please know God is still writing His glory in my story. He is using my life as *A Planted Tree: Creating His* **PATH** *To Freedom.*

See you all later at the House.